Wild Sweet Orange Ride

Journeys Home

Julia Gregg

Vineyard Stories
Edgartown, Massachussetts

Volume Copyright ©2014 Julia Gregg

Published by Vineyard Stories
52 Bold Meadow Road
Edgartown, MA 02539
508 221 2338
www.vineyardstories.com

Images pages 10 and 46 ©2014 Linda Waren Goodridge
Images pages 24, 64, and 84 ©2014 Janice Glass

Library of congress: 2014942089
ISBN: 978-0-9915028-4-4

Book Design: Jill Dible, Atlanta, GA

Printed in China

Contents

Searching for Sun

Trial by Fire

Shifting Wind

Revived by Water

Finding Air

Introduction

THE ROAD THAT BEGINS with leaving all we have known, renouncing the familiar, and searching for an individual place in the sun can lead to great travels, complete with jarring off-road detours.

Inevitably there are mistakes, regrets, and trials, but after some time, winds can shift, and even the most stubborn and headstrong (lessons learned) can find peace—albeit a peace that rests on contradiction and complexity.

This is a collection about the search for place. The paradox that comes with the tenderest of our loves—for regions, for passions, for our children or our mates—is that the most wonderful experiences can also be the most searing. If we are willing to be open to an introspective journey, we can learn, finally, to balance and to breathe.

I believe that alienation and hurt are healed by unconditional love and friendship, by work accomplished with pride, and by art—words well written, music shared, or other artistic creations which reassure that we are all part of a singular puzzling human journey.

Many thanks to all who believed that rendering this sometimes bitter, mostly sweet ride might build bridges to others. That includes editors at the *Evansville Courier and Press* who first published some pieces in this collection. Special thanks to artists Janice Glass Williams, who shared the vision, and Linda Goodridge, who made permanent the memory of beloved beach dwellings. Deep appreciation goes to editor and publisher Jan Pogue of Vineyard Stories for her artistic eye and belief in bringing this book to life.

"Memory is a complicated thing, a relative to truth, but not its twin."
—BARBARA KINGSOLVER

Searching
for Sun

Montgomery, Alabama

THE EARLY PLACES, the first places, seep into the skin and mind and heart like humidity into a salt box until the salt cannot be dried nor the water extracted, and both remain, for better or worse, in a bonded clump.

Rules and tradition form a tangle that mixes with gardenia smells, overgrown vegetation, and oppressive heat, and knotted at the center of the muddle is the most peculiar of the Southern flora, the family tree. Branch after branch (some bearing no resemblance whatsoever to any other) drops down like Banyan roots, disparate and inescapable.

Years later, when the tangle is unknotted, a breeze blows through the opened spaces, sending words and memory like delicate sticks and leaves

skittering

across the page. . . .

Finley Avenue

A HUGE PORCH, shaded by banana and camellia bushes, half circled the house on Finley Avenue. Like a partial moat, the porch (accessible by ten wide concrete steps) sheltered the imposing Alabama residence and its strange inhabitants. Inside lived Crazy Harry, fat-armed Gonga (and her liver-eating cat, Prissy), Aunt Ruth and her silent, sullen husband—all relatives, now stacked in one dark, crowded memory tomb.

My mother told us, "You need to visit Gonga . . . and don't wear shorts. She doesn't like shorts." To me she added, "Don't whistle! A whistling girl and a cackling hen always come to the same sad end." When my brothers and I climbed the formidable steps at our mother's command, we were inevitably met—not by our great-grandmother, Gonga, with her toothless, gummy smile—but by the vivid red lipstick and dyed black hair of our great-aunt Ruth. But, thank God, it wasn't *Uncle Harry* . . . never-married, scary Harry, tossing us up over his massive, furry shoulders. When I grew up and ventured to make light of our most terrifying moments with Harry, my youngest brother, Jeff, reminded me that Harry was no joke—then or now. And Gonga, much kinder in her massive sickbed and darkened room, wasn't that funny either. The memories of her gas heater, liver-stained cat plates, and wrinkled, flabby arms still evoke a moment of silence.

So it was that the house on Finley Avenue came to be one of my first mentally inescapable homeplaces. I still dream of it, its November windfall pecans scattered across a perpetually green and brown yard, its November camellias hanging limp in the first frost. Within sight, across a side street, my favorite grandmother's red-shingled house beckoned like a flare: *Safe House! Hot Cheese Toast and Chili Here! Whistling Allowed.*

Several miles away, my paternal grandmother's formal Victorian house on Sayre Street waited somewhat snobbishly for my visits, and the space that separated the Sayre Street house from the tribe on Finley Avenue seemed, through my childish eyes, interminably great. In reality, my mother's and father's extended families harbored themselves within relatively short distances of each other, and my first ideas of homeplaces were rooted, old Southern dwellings. As Faulkner observed about similar Mississippi structures, they lifted their "coquettish decay" above modern Southern progress that was fast encroaching.

When I dream at night, this half-century later, the house on Finley and the wooden house on Sayre are still standing—and for sale—in their original quiet neighborhoods, and I'm wrestling with the decision to return and remodel or stay states away from the stifling heat and terrible chore of rebuilding. When I wake, I realize both houses have been physically obliterated. It is a psychological mystery that I keep looking for them. Certainly, their inhabitants cannot be idealized into soul mates I need to revisit, nor would their refurbished selves match the dreams I have of them. Yet for every move I've made, and there have been dozens, the houses left behind cry out like ghosts for reconciliation—for some closure of my leaving. They say, "You can move on, but we'll follow you, waiting in the shadows; we'll come to you at night when you have no option of closing us away; we'll visit in white-wooden dreams to remind you of that time, just before nightfall, when lightning bugs climbed curved banisters and sticky heat burned who you are into your soul."

Decatur Street Exit

MY MOTHER, A practical, legalistic, fundamental Christian woman—born and raised in Alabama—told me once while we were eating seafood, years after my only child was born, that she thought her mother might have been reincarnated into my son. She thought so, she said, because my grandmother had loved and favored me, and near the end of her life, when memories and desires became confused, my grandmother had wanted to come live with me. After that bombshell, my mother went on eating her flounder and never mentioned it again.

I think of this now, decades after leaving Alabama, as I travel fast through Montgomery, noticing how unruly the highway medians are. All the weeds and vegetation along the road form something like a crazy quilt, with none of the studied care of yards in the Midwest where I now live and work.

Very little is fastidiously cared for in the Deep South. Somehow, grass, trees, and shrubs are simply too incorrigible—and the weather too hot—to struggle with the clover and stickers and vines that are never killed out by winter. The roadsides remain green, even this far past summer, and camellias droop against dark tangles where undergrowth looks ancient and deserving of being left alone. In spring, wisteria crawls up the azalea and gardenia bushes and drops its purple scent on the humid air, but now the air is October dry. I am noticing the medians and yards, and so I drive far past the center of town.

I could turn around.

I could exit and visit the cemetery as I've considered, or I could exit and drive past Grandmother Cook's house on Decatur Street.

So many years have gone by; could I find my way?

I want to see the front porch again, painted barn-red, with cracks in the concrete that slither to the screen door. But there is something about Montgomery that unsettles me. So in my car I drive ahead.

In my mind, I turn around, remembering *Wagon Train* in a room lit by black-and-white flickers. I press my eight-year-old forehead against the dusty metal screen door to watch, but I'm not ready to go inside. Instead, I tap dance on the pyracantha berry-red concrete, keeping time with the brass section of the high school band that sounds across the night sky from the stadium. Later, I will climb into my grandmother's double bed and watch the headlights from busy Decatur Street crawl eerily around the bedroom wall, and I will be safe.

In this night's memory, however, I cannot sleep. "Grandmother," I say into the dark. "I've done something wrong." Silence.

"When I was buying ice cream, I broke a glass toy on the turnaround rack. It crashed on the floor." Still she does not answer me, but she gets up in a night interrupted by horns and headlights from the busy street and pulls on her housedress and sweater. I do the same. She takes my hand, and we cross the concrete porch, down the stone steps, past the phlox, and, hand in hand, we head down the dusty side path that borders Decatur Street.

It is two blocks to the 7-Eleven. Open until eleven, it is still brightly lit. We go in, and I tell the clerk what I have done. My grandmother pays him sixty-nine cents. She never scolds or lectures. She says only, "You must pay what you owe."

We tread up the dusty path to her steps, her barn-red porch, back through her screen door. We undress and slide beneath a silky red comforter, and she holds my hand. In summer, the comforter will be replaced with a light, calico spread, but for now we are safe and warm under feathers and satin.

My grandmother Cook saves and spends carefully. In a dozen years she will pay my sorority dues and buy clothes for me so that I "can be like the other girls." An orphan herself, she knows how isolation feels. She will lend me money when I need it, and I will pay her back, $41 at a time.

In two dozen years she will be gone. I will fly home to her funeral, and my luggage will be lost along the way. I will stand in the Alabama January cold, wearing only a cotton dress, boots, and an old sweater that belonged to her. It will seem clear to me in the January yellow sun, in the blue cold of the cemetery, that I should have a child, that I should pass on her lessons and love. I will be more than thirty years old, and the thought of having children will never have seriously occurred to me before.

I am driving fast on Interstate 65, and I have gone too far to turn back to the cemetery exit. I have gone too far to buy $41 worth of flowers to place on my grandmother's grave. I have gone too far to turn around, exit onto Court Street and then Decatur, too far to be disillusioned by the porch, chipped and peeling, by the screen door, torn. But I have not gone too far to outrace the nagging remembrance that I might not have paid the last $41 I owed her of a $410 college loan.

It comes to me, clearly, what must be done. When I get to Indiana, hours from now, I will steal into my son's dark room, a room far out into the suburbs—too safe to be visited by city noise and crawling headlights. I will say, "Help him to know love." Tucking the cover that belonged to my grandmother close around him, I will slide three folded bills, two twenties and a one, beneath his pillow. I will say into the night, "Maybe I owe this." Then, "Bless my child and keep him safe. Help him to know honesty."

I will wonder in the tired, dark night if we ever pay our debts or know our places in an infinite cosmos of ethereal and real.

Tunneling Through

YEARS HAVE PASSED, but the image is clear and persistent. She is tiny and blonde, with glasses. I am coerced into remembering that her mother, Lurleen, died in the spring of 1968. Men in uniforms came for her at play practice. In the deep, quiet, dark Alabama night, as we practiced *Bye Bye Birdie*, state troopers came into the high school auditorium and called Peggy Wallace away. More images assault me. My heart is sinking, breaking for her; my eyes are wide, but I do not speak.

How does a person lose a parent when spring is in the night air and everything is so young? Her heart seems gentle enough that a loss this heavy could smother it. One year later in the spring, I learn something about how she managed to breathe under such a loss. My father dies, and sorting through the stacks of cards after his death, I find a letter to my mother from Peggy's dad, Governor George Wallace.

He writes personal words, on state stationery under a gold seal, to comfort us in our loss, his own still fresh.

WHAT ABOUT OTHER LOSSES? Voices scream, and placards shout: I HAVE A DREAM! ALABAM, YOU'VE GOT YOUR WHEEL IN A DITCH.

I am remembering a shy girl with glasses and a soft voice. When people ask what her father does, she says merely that he works for the state. There are other faces, as dark as Peggy's is light. Nineteen sixty-eight, power changing hands. There were a dozen stunning moments when we knew, internalized, that change was personal and real for all of us, black and white alike, change directed mostly by others—federal judges, politicians, movers and shakers—many of whom would be able to walk away while we'd be left to sift through the ashes, confused and chaotic, the same as 100 years before.

Power changing hands breeds anger and violence, no matter what the time or place. I am remembering the sadness in my mother's voice after the bussing had come and gone, after the knives appeared in public school restrooms and all who could afford the change had moved their children to safer ground, private schools.

My mother writes: "I pass a band practice field and see what remains of a once-proud tradition, now practicing in thin, straggling lines. What has happened to our schools? Our lives?"

Was this the price of merging? If so, it was the price we had to pay for being on the wrong side of history and humanity.

But can any of us physically go back if we finally find a way out? And can we ever find a way out unless we face the tasks of tunneling through, understanding the disorder?

Delores

THE RESPONSE FROM Delores Boyd is polite but hurried. She isn't sure if she remembers me. She will look me up in the high school yearbook. Days later our tenuous relationship is confirmed. She sends me my 1967 yearbook inscription, all these years later, across miles of time and space. She does recall who I was—one of the few, she says, who had neither taunted her nor looked through her as if she were not there.

I do not need to see her picture in a stained and crumbling yearbook. I remember her clearly. She has been a force shaping who I have become, and I have carried the picture of her courage with me for years. Some of the details have been lost: for example, was she the first black student brought into our school of twenty-six hundred whites? Was she escorted by federal marshals, as Vivian Malone at the University of Alabama had been several years before? These things I don't see as vividly as I see her sitting next to me in chemistry class. She never spoke unless she was addressed; she was refined and intelligent. I remember when I first spoke to her.

When the time came for my senior parties, I requested that Delores be included on the guest list, and my parents said no. This I remember most of all.

Some of the things from that terrible time when Martin Luther King preached in our city and Freedom Riders passed through our streets might be mixed now with imagination. There is this mental picture of Rosa Parks as she is taken away by police on the local nightly news. Did I dream that the woman was dragged in black-and-white off my TV screen by men several times her size? This I remember with exactness:

TV crews covered our church services, and ushers refused to let "colored people" enter because it was against God's plan.

I have now evolved in my limited understanding of possible plans . . . and in my understanding of other people. But the wisdom of institutions—family, church—diminish, marred by the illogical and disturbing.

In my late thirties I reconnect with Delores, and in the first letters that follow, I learn that, besides being a successful attorney and judge, Delores co-owns a bookstore, that we admire many of the same authors, and that Alice Walker has held a reading at the bookstore she owns. I am impressed. I write my once and future acquaintance, Delores Boyd: We could have been real friends, I tell her. I know it is never too late; our paths can cross again. Perhaps they are inextricably crossed already.

I revisit accounts of the lives of Rosa Parks, Lurleen Wallace, and Vivian Malone. I discover Hurston and Alice Walker. I reread Jesse Jackson, Robert Kennedy, and Martin Luther King. All of us have paid a price for learning and living in a time when humankind has been evolving upward. For some the price has been death of the body and for some a thousand deaths of the heart. I am realizing that this lifetime has been a pathway, covered with regret . . . moving toward a more enlightened place?

I recognize that Delores, at sixteen years old, faced hundreds of people who did not look like her or think like her or know her at all. She turned her back on taunts and hostility and closed her eyes when rich white Southern girls with half her intelligence and spirit looked right through her as if she were not there—when boys threw milk cartons, aimed at her head and heart.

Her presence changed our school, and her example taught more than I could have learned in books. What I learned most of all is this: An individual life of courage can begin to change the world.

Grayton Beach / December

THE ROADS LEADING to the Red Bar are beach lanes, lined by old wooden summer houses and twisted scrub oaks. Thick fog sits on everything—like cotton along the north Florida highways—billowy, white, and full. The gnarled fingers of the trees, whose roots dig their toes only into sand, hold up the fog like scarves around their arms, and the night, at first, is silent.

All day three friends and I have driven from Indiana, across Kentucky, and then down I-65 toward the Gulf Coast, looking for sun, passing the time by trying to guess artists on the oldies station before anyone else in the car can pry the right singing group out of some obscure dustbin of the brain.

Driving through Montgomery, the place I was born and raised, I don't even guess The Temptations because I am lost in a reverie of hearing old lyrics in the exact geographical location where I heard them decades ago. I am suddenly eighteen, transported to 1968, remembering all the reasons I had to leave Alabama.

I close my eyes and feel bursts of orange from the sun, as we pass trucks, pine trees, road signs, exits—through Montgomery and out again.

My friends and I have eaten our way south: turnip greens, boiled peanuts, and—finally—donuts when we hit Pensacola and see the HOT light flashing in the Krispy Kreme window. Once inside, asking directions to the restroom, I am sent to the rear loading dock where the doors are flung open to the warm gray air. At the very back, among stacked and scattered boxes, a man in a stained apron rests on an overturned container reading the newspaper.

"This can't possibly be the way to the restroom," I say.

"Oh, yeah, honey, it is. Go on in through there."

So I wind my way into the entrails of a workroom coated in flour and find a restroom that, by Midwestern standards of cleanliness, would likely be condemned. Through the open back doors, I can see camellia bushes and a lone woman in a cotton house dress limping down the sidewalk, I suppose toward home.

I have always imagined that I would be that woman, going home someday to the South; I would carve a space for myself in the world and make friends in other places who would become family. But when I grew older, limping—perhaps not literally—I imagined being drawn toward what I'd known growing up: warm evenings with twilight shining purple (like light through stained glass) behind the pink of the crabapple trees.

But no decade's journey has unraveled as planned, and I have lived long enough in this mobile global village to realize that I'm home wherever my heart and mind are connected and at peace. I am grounded by a certain central core, my own inner strength that hardened when foolishness, loss, and adversity made character building essential. Grow or die. Move forward and try again to connect.

On this December night, once out of Pensacola, we pass through Fort Walton and Destin until we're finally traveling down County Road 283. Out of the silence, music begins to creep across the air. We turn the corner where the asphalt ends, drops off into the ocean, and the Red Bar lights up the night like a beckoning harlot, dressed in scarlet and yellow. Music blares and people spill out of the open door into the warm Florida night where the lights are garish against the dark. Just another December night in a Southern beach town; I feel at home. And isn't this what we travel all our lives to feel?

Trial by Fire

Tennessee Memory

For my son

AUTUMN IN NASHVILLE is turquoise and feathers, boots and leather, in a city ringed with hills in sweater colors.

In a photo of a farm in twilight woods, golden light hugs you in, surrounds you there on your pony, in your cowboy hat. You smile into the camera, and I remember that as a little boy, you loved me over-much.

We carved pumpkins and sugared violets and tramped the hills, and I readied you for a time when you would stroll away, seldom looking back. You learned independence well, slipping through my fingers before the last lessons could commence.

Parenting has been a crucible, burning away all pride and pretense, leaving only what is real: such effort and hope and tenderness.

> *All as it should be . . .*
> *Still, I try to recall just once*
> *from a time so long ago*
> *when your hand rested*
> *in mine.*

Mind-Sieve

I REMEMBER THE TIME before nightfall in a summer street of children and bikes, when the radio played *West Side Story* and we drew hopscotch grids with chalk. It is the dusk that lingers, all these years later—dusk blue and still, with no wind moving across the porches where bathrobed women water evening shrubs.

I remember the hot wind playing in the trees behind my grandmother's house; in very late September the heat would wither out, and the sun would slant a different way through yellow-green leaves that were slow to make way for autumn. It is the slant of the sun that I remember most, a sign that summer was coming to a slow, dry end.

When I call back the important times of childhood, it is not the births or deaths, the warnings or gifts, or even the lessons I remember; it is the feeling about seasons and people.

For children, characters are never rounded, whole people with histories and hurts, with motives and hidden sides beneath their surfaces; personalities are not, for a child, complex and multifaceted. Children remember only one side of the people they know, the side that is turned toward them.

We carry forward memories of nature and human nature, sifted through a child's mind-sieve. There is the late night when, drawn close to a warm and constant grandmother, the child watches headlights crawl their eerie way across the wall, and forever the lights are burned there in the dark next to the memory of safety and unending patience.

There is a Zen saying: Human feelings are frail; the ways of the world are rugged. And since I cannot know what will be remembered, especially by children who have their own ways of sifting and sorting, I try to encourage larger stores of love and beauty from which later they may choose.

Summer nights fall around the children in this neighborhood, farther north and cooler than the neighborhoods I knew. Boys run through the yard, playing bloody murder. Last year, they trampled down my daises and hid in the plum tree, knocking off the leaves. I spoke to them about that.

This year they stay out too late and chase through a black velvet night in dark clothes, and when my son comes in, he puts wet, dirty sweatpants in the hamper to mildew. I find them days later and think of lecturing—bringing up last year's daises—and insisting that he take responsibility for his own laundry.

I am the adult now, and Zach is the one unconsciously storing memories of all that is full and warm and good about summer and the slant of sun that comes before the dusk—blue and still.

I wash loads of smelly clothes and clean mud out of cleats. I buy new bike tire tubes and rollerblade wheels. I decide against lectures on cleaning mud out of bearings and preventing mildew in clothes hampers. I space my battles carefully.

Something of this summer, clothed in its own feeling, will be brought back again and again by a muddy boy with daisy petals stuck in his cleats. And he will bear pictures of his heart's growing or dying away—pictures I have helped to paint—all throughout his life.

Losses

THERE ARE SO MANY ways of leaving, so many ways of being left, that I cannot commit them all to memory, much less to paper.

When my son was beginning school, loss followed loss: a move from our beloved Tennessee hills, a divorce, the death of our dog Deege. Coming home from school one day, out of nowhere, Zach finally cried, large tears resting on the ends of his lashes.

"I miss Deege," Zach said. I have learned over the years that the first loss mentioned is the scab on a wound that goes much deeper.

I reached for his hand. "Me, too." Tears dripped down to wet my collar, and we sat riding like that, silent.

He hadn't cried when I'd led his dog away. He'd chosen not to go with me to the vet.

All the way from the north side of town to the west, the big dog had lain next to me, his paw resting in my hand. That's the way he'd always been, heading for the vet; he'd become a big baby, lifting his heavy paw to be held. He'd wait, sure I'd be beside him in whatever he had to endure.

We'd gotten Deege (real name, D.O.G., accent on the O) to comfort Zach when we'd first moved to Evansville. Then we had been a family of three. Daily I'd watched ads in the paper to find a part-shepherd, like the one we'd had to leave behind in Tennessee. "I miss my dog," he'd say in a five-year-old voice, confused about his first real loss. And I, of course, tried to make things right.

We found, finally, D.O.G., a gentle, well-trained country dog. His owners complained that he'd learned to chase sheep from a stray and so had become a liability on their farm. They loved him but couldn't keep him, and so their five-year-old dog came to live with our five-year-old son.

The huge dog followed Zach everywhere. When he would head down the street to play basketball, Deege would amble along beside him. When Zach went into a neighbor's house to play, Deege waited patiently, obstructing the neighbor's doorway until his buddy returned from inside.

When Zach was old enough to ride the bus, D.O.G. followed him to the bus stop and embarrassed him daily by trying to board the bus. The driver would scold Zach, and the little boy would lift the massive paws down from the bus steps and send his big dog on his way. But Deege could hear the afternoon sound of the bus returning, and he'd race to the stop, and there he'd be again.

I am a working mother. I've only seen my son disembark from a school bus once—only once in all his years in school. On that one occasion, I held my breath to see them all there in a line, the neighborhood children and one big hairy dog with a curled tail, all laughing or smiling, even Deege (he could smile), and I cried then at the simple beauty of it all.

D.O.G. had intuitive sense (or scents) about him. He'd dig a place below the window of any room in which I slept; when visitors came, moving me from my regular room, he moved, too, and he rested under the window of my rearranged location, a regal protection.

There are so many things to remember about Deege, the way he'd nudge our little blind Yorkie home when she would wander away, the way he kissed and played with his tiny friend. Deege had wonderful manners; he'd never eat when people were watching, no matter how hungry he might be, and he never complained when we dressed him in Ninja Turtle noses on Halloween.

Halloweens came and went, mostly all the same, but this last Halloween seemed to mark a passage. Zach knelt beside his dog, not clad in costume; he'd grown too old for that. This year there was just a boy and a dog and a mask. My friend took their picture.

This Halloween Deege moved more slowly.

The weather grew colder, and D.O.G. found it harder and harder to dig himself a space outside my window. He circled painfully and could hardly lower himself to rest. One day Zach and I returned to find him collapsed in our neighbors' yard. They were standing watch over him, but he couldn't get to his feet. Then I knew.

I would have to take him to the vet one final time; I would hold his paw in my hand, and he would trust me to make him well, but I would be forced to leave him.

When the day came, the vet would not let me come inside to hold him. I felt like a traitor. I abandoned him there and went away to cry alone.

Our Yorkie, that little bug of a dog, searched for her big, gentle friend for weeks. There was his bowl; there was the place he slept outside. Where had he gone?

Zach remained silent as she searched, silent each time we returned home with no greeting, no wagging of the tail. We ran and bicycled without our usual companion, accompanied by an empty space we never talked about. Two months passed.

Yesterday we sat crying together in the car, crying for all of our losses: the move, a family that broke apart two years later, a beloved pet. I found no words to tell Zach that life is complex and fragile and I don't know how to fix everything.

Today, I found myself surprised by the holiday pictures I picked up from the photo shop. There, among the expected shots (the snow, Zach's birthday, Christmas), D.O.G. stared up at me from under an autumn sun. Next to him knelt a boy, green Halloween mask in hand, and both the boy and the dog were smiling. Are smiling. Stilled in time.

I took the autumn photo from the packet and placed it in a bright red frame in Zachary's room. I want to tell him, "I'll keep you safe from loss," but I'm fairly certain he knows I can't. I haven't.

There are some things a parent cannot fix. Even with love.

Love is no stitch for a gaping hole, but it is a salve.

Soccer

I WANT TO TELL my son: Someday, if all goes well, you will have a child of your own to take to a new beginning of school.

It will be one of those crisp mornings in August, before the September heat pours yellow over a long ending-of-summer, and you will watch your child walk away from you to his first day of school—elementary, high school, whatever—it doesn't matter; the feeling will be the same. You will notice as he travels away from you that he needs a haircut and that he's growing taller and thinner. You will notice that he carries a part of your heart with him when he goes, though he doesn't know it's there, and if he did, he'd brush it off in embarrassment without looking back at you, watching from the car.

This August morning is burned into the part of my brain that is my heart. The trees are deep green; the air is cool, and the sky is far off and blue, not heavy and closing in. You walk with three friends toward the gate where soccer tryout results are posted.

You are all beginning to be men—not the bantering, silly middle school kids you were. Your barbs at one another are clever and funny, but I know beneath the humor is anticipation and dread.

What if one of you—or more—doesn't make the team? How will you turn around with your bags and water bottles and walk back to the car with your friends watching?

I know you are tense; I am, too. My shoulders knot, and I watch from my place in the driver's seat.

Together, for weeks, the four of you have gone to conditioning in a new high school, and I have warned you: Think before you speak; try your hardest, but be cautious as a newcomer.

Soon you will walk into a new school with some identity in place; once there, it will change and grow. Have I helped to give you roots and strength to be secure? (What is this complex obsession with roots and community from an individual who has valued only autonomy?) Perhaps I want for those I love what has been hard for me to find.

Just this once I hope for the transition to be easier, for you to enter as a member of a team, a group.

A boy returns to the van parked in front of me. "I didn't make it," he says to the woman waiting there.

The four of you peer over shoulders at the list on the gate. I hold my breath. You finally nod and casually wave me away. You seem irritated when I hold up four fingers in a questioning gesture. Yes, you nod again; we all made the team.

You hurry off.

I pull away from the soccer field and notice with surprise that I am crying. I have a sense of time's moving on, but I don't know if I feel loss or gain; I know I feel relief.

I want to give you this Elizabeth Stone quote: "To have a child . . . is to decide forever to have your heart go walking around outside your body."

But now is clearly not the time.

Besides, someday you'll know that for yourself . . . if all goes well.

Solitary Burden

AT DUSK IN COZUMEL, Mexico, people saunter along narrow streets and music lifts over the palms, floating to a navy sky that touches the shore in a pink line. A dance recital is progressing on center stage of the town square. Honeybee dancers, finished with their performance, sit with ice cream and beautiful dark-skinned mothers.

It is spring break. I miss my beloved Florida coast, but I try to immerse myself in this new adventure. I have gone at the insistence of those I care about.

Mexico is a country of contrasts, of color and surprises. Plain black birds descend from palm trees and startle with unexpected blue wings and yellow beaks. Gray iguanas sun themselves in camouflage and then rustle away in agitation across green and yellow grass.

We've rented a red Jeep and bumped along back-beach roads in the heat and wind, but now the breeze is still, and we navigate the Wrangler down stone streets at twilight. I can touch the people next to me at stop signs, old women on scooters, families walking arm-in-arm across sidewalks, but, of course, I don't. Instead, I smile and stare.

We drive past beauty parlors with no storefronts and sidewalk groceries in bright rows. All are open to the evening air. Florists show off colorful plants, shaped like so many tropical birds behind the window glass.

At restaurants families eat with relish, with gusto and laughter. The men are attentive to their children, and I recall a passage from Mexican American writer Richard Rodriguez about the contrast of Mexico and America: "Mexico has been the happier place for being a country of tragedy. Tragic cultures serve up better food than optimistic cultures; tragic cultures have sweeter children, more opulent funerals. In tragic cultures, one does not bear the solitary burden of optimism."

I think I understand what he means about the solitary burden of optimism. In my own family, as soon as possible, each child, for generations, has headed off to college and to a new life, never thinking about turning back or asking for help past a certain point. We have each believed that anything is possible, based on individual strength of spirit, intelligence, and ambition. We are a stubborn and self-reliant crew, sometimes disconnected for all our bravado.

Rodriguez suggests that those who know poverty, fragility, and hardship stick together, relishing the joys and ceremony that inevitably come with gratitude. Those who face difficulty, he suggests, value the important moments.

I am remembering the reverent tone of Rodriguez's writing as sunset wraps this Mexican island in indigo light. This is a country of contrasts and surprises, a poor country of rich beauty, an old country with much to teach me about the importance of connection.

Floating Free

IT IS ALMOST too late when I decide to teach my son the value of community. I have been so busy instructing him to soar, to follow his passions, that I have neglected to teach him the value of all that grounds us. In his senior year of high school, I decide that he needs to understand something about his roots . . . not just his Midwestern roots, formed in the last dozen years of his life, but my Southern roots that have made me who I am, and therefore made him who he is. I want him to understand what I have both cherished and rejected, held onto and pushed against.

We will be visiting my acquaintance, Delores Boyd, in Montgomery. He will be interviewing her for a school project, and I will be continuing to try to build a friendship. I think I know some of what she went through in the civil rights violence of 1968 and surrounding years because I was there. But once again, her dignity and insight will teach me how little I have known.

When we arrive at her law office in historic Montgomery, she is gracious, as always. Many of her answers to his questions are expected, familiar. But when Zach asks how it felt to be ostracized in her high school of twenty-six hundred whites and only a dozen other black students, her answer stuns me: "Well, it was of little concern. I went home to a very rich community that met in the evenings with Martin Luther King, Ralph Abernathy, and others. I was supported by parents and community who were strong. Lanier [our high school] meant only an education for me. I knew where I was going."

Imagine my continued, hollow belief, all these decades, that we whites at Sidney Lanier High School had something to give her. Acceptance perhaps? What arrogance. While our belief systems, paradigms, and community were in many ways crumbling, she had had the moral ascendency, the community, the support.

As a high school teacher for many years, I have told my students that graduation year is one of the most memorable of life. We all leave what we know and head into a new world. For me, graduation year meant the deaths of Bobby Kennedy, Martin Luther King Jr., and Governor Lurleen Wallace; Vietnam War unrest; and an Auburn University campus that was amazingly untouched by political turmoil. For Zach, 2001 meant freedom from Midwestern restrictions, weeks of walking the streets of New York City, knowing almost no one, and the September 2001 attack on the World Trade Center. He watched the buildings fall from his vantage point on the Brooklyn Bridge.

The losses we sustain and the history we live when we are young take years to process and decode. Zach and I have flailed about, trying urgently to get out of all that binds us, and we have paid a price for floating free.

Homeplaces, Next Generation

YEARS AGO, A PALE print hanging in a San Francisco bookstore captivated me, and I went to some trouble to obtain it and have it matted and framed. The print is the cover of *Homeplaces, Stories of the South by Women Writers*, edited by Mary Ellis Gibson, and it shows a white clapboard house identical to my paternal grandmother's, except for the actual numbers on the address placard nailed above the mailbox. The artist is Kip Gerard.

Standing in that San Francisco bookstore, I was intensely aware that many of us spend our lifetimes searching for homeplaces—places where we feel connected. My son Zach, interviewed in 2000 for a TV special, impressed the New York interviewer with what she termed "a confident, youthful edge." She asked for his impressions of his hometown, and he replied that it didn't move quite fast enough for him. Searching for colleges, he implied that I, his mother (who groomed him for independence and open-mindedness), might not understand his need to experience the world—that I might not fully grasp his "need" to explore colleges in New York since I seem so content with "home." I asked him to consider my alma mater, Auburn, and he dismissed both the South and the Midwest with youthful disdain.

So he must find his way, too.

My contentment, I want to tell him, has been a long time coming. I have threaded my way up and down Interstate 65, trying on lifestyles without knowing what I sought. I've taken lessons in life (and in colleges) in Alabama, Florida, Tennessee, Kentucky, and Indiana, and I know well what he is seeking in New York—himself, unfettered.

He is seeking a place of peace and possibility and acceptance.

So go, I tell him. Send me the bills, and I will pay as many of them as I can; you will find a way to pay the rest. Send me news of ideas, searches, anger, growth, and change. Look for someone to hold your hand and heart—someone to touch your mind and spirit.

Gather all you can, I say—here in the spring of your vibrant, broiling life. I will be waiting in warm September, in Indian summer, learning to let go.

Mirror

I HALT IN THE DRIVEWAY where I am pacing with the phone pressed to my ear. I strain to hear every nuanced word across a night filled with insect sounds and blackness.

"I don't have a family that protects me," my son says. This is a new twist to an old discussion.

And it's at least partially true—a psychological epiphany for him and for me. That's exactly how I felt about my own parents and my missing, idealized extended family: No reunions, no uncles or grandfathers with sound advice and insurance policies. Does anyone have that? And what is the price of such connection and expectation?

He is raving, hurt, and angry. He returns to the black hole of our divorced family. He is uncertain of his place, doesn't have a clear path. I say across all the cities and states that crowd the miles between us that he is independent, beautiful and intelligent, sensitive and fully alive in a world that doesn't offer certainties.

I am pacing again, assuring him that his is a common anxiety for an introspective person. I am silent for a moment before I tell him, "We are mirrors, you and I. I learn who I have been by looking into you." We are the first in this family to try this hard to understand each other across generational divides; I am sure of it.

There are deeper things I do not say because they are irrelevant for someone who has never loved a child. I don't say that I bring in every plant he has sent for long-distance gifts, nurse them through winter, setting them out again to flourish every spring . . . that I save them year to year as if some life or love depended on it.

I don't say that I tremble at his disapproval just as he trembles at mine. And all those times I acted angry and indignant, I was really just afraid.

There are things we never say because emotion is just too tender and taut and we're trying to keep our heads above water in the presence of those who touch the deepest of our love and bruises.

This is not the right time to confide that I'm sorry I was so foolish and arrogant and dismissive of my own parents, to admit that by the time I quit fighting for independence and identity, it was too late to talk to someone no longer there.

For some families, loving and laughing seem easy and spontaneous, but for others the beauty or hurt of a moment never makes it to discussion; it simmers as poem or prose or painting, a memory committed only to paper. But that's a family, too—the one that has a deep, hard time finding and keeping connection.

Researchers at Tufts University and the New England Medical Center in Boston have discovered that mothers carry their children's fetal cells inside their bodies for decades, even a lifetime, after the baby is born. The cells rest there, unattended, but undeniably lurking.

I knew it, of course, before research. It's as if mothers and children are connected by some golden filament, "stretched to airy thinness" as John Donne describes it, connected across time and space . . . children on one end of the golden thread and we on the other.

As our children grow, the old roles we have worn are shed and scatter like dry dust, but our connection hovers along the golden line that stretches, thinner and thinner, between us.

I don't say any of this to him, nor do I say that I've been scrambling for years to fill in the blanks for both of us, to make a "real family," to find my way with genes so stubborn and independent that I probably wouldn't have taken advice or help had it been offered. Why do we have to learn everything through hard experience?

But I do say this: "I love you more than life itself, as you once told me." There are signs we have to learn to read—gifts, apologies, the opening of a heart onto a page.

I do say, "You have a family that protects you," but I don't explain that I see myself teetering out on a limb, balancing him on the tip of a wobbling finger that I hold out to the sun. Take the light, I pray daily; find the air.

He would never hear it if I explained: This is what we do here in this life, listen for hours on the phone to someone we love who is searching for sense and sun and roots. And we hold on to one another lest we fall apart.

Until we find a part.

The Kindness of Strangers

BECAUSE OF A LONG DELAY in Nashville, I miss a connecting flight. I am transferred to another airline, booked on a flight into Atlanta, and finally slide into my airline row, thankful to be beside an empty seat. I read and try not to think. I am on my way to Florida to see my youngest brother who has been diagnosed with a cancer so advanced that there is no treatment. I am frazzled and fragile, but our family does not appreciate "fragile," and so I am reading instead of falling apart.

When the plane lands in Atlanta, I open the overhead bin and struggle unsuccessfully with my carry-on bag, surprised when a young man behind me offers to help and hands the bag down to me. I am so touched by the kindness of this stranger that I finally cry, heavy tears streaking silently down my face as I exit ahead of him.

I have been reading *Winter Journal* by Paul Auster, which opens with these lines: "You think it will never happen to you, that it cannot happen to you, that you are the only person in the world to whom none of these things will ever happen, and then, one by one, they all begin to happen to you, in the same way they happen to everyone else."

At breakfast before my trip, two friends, who are both caring for parents with Alzheimer's, in addition to caring for their own children, alternately break into tears. Each has a stressful job, runs a home, and assumes the task of reminding her parent daily that his or her spouse is no longer alive. "Don't you remember?" they say, and, "Yes, this is the house where you live. This is your home." I listen to both friends with silent, bewildered respect at their resilience. The only thing that I can give is empathy.

Here, I could cite the alarming statistics about the prevalence of Alzheimer's and cancer, but statistics seem irrelevant. What seems relevant is this: In the end, nothing much matters except friendship and sensitivity to the burdens other people carry. Coping and character and kindness seem relevant.

When it comes time for me to drive to the Nashville airport, one of my breakfast friends offers to drive with me, and I accept.

In Florida I find that my brother is much worse than I could have imagined. I take him to the beach, but he can no longer see well, and so I guide him slowly, arm in arm. At some point he drops his medication, and when I go back to the spot where I think it might be, a truck has parked there. I am certain that I look ridiculous trying to find a small white pill next to the vast stretch of sand. The man in the pickup asks if he can help. I hesitate to tell him about the pill, about my brother who cannot see to find it, but, in the end, I do tell him, and he looks until he spots it. I thank him, feeling grateful out of proportion for another small act of kindness.

What is it about difficulty, the kind of difficulty that you do not see coming, that tenderizes the heart?

Difficulty that you think "will never happen to you" heightens sensitivity and straightens priorities, and when difficulty that "cannot happen to you" does happen, an invisible net of friendship and universal connection, of common concern and kindness, stretches to hold us up.

Haven

WHEN RAIN SLASHES against window glass, bookstore lights are especially warm and welcoming. Inside, where sounds and scents are soft, colored designs of book covers stack against one another, richly artistic—like paintings in a gallery.

Offering coffee and quiet, bookstores present the pleasant illusion that the world retains a degree of order, even when sanity and sequence can hardly be verified.

On the shelves, strewn across reading tables and left in the corners of cushy chairs, words sleep, folded against each other in phrases, waiting to wake, string together and uncoil, connecting mind to mind like so much
   electrical wiring
      unfurling.

Monroeville, Alabama

I AM ON ANOTHER of my literary treks, deep into the South, off Interstate 65, to Monroeville, Alabama. My companions remind me that at the end of our search in Florida for the birthplace of African American folklorist and novelist Zora Neale Hurston we found only a rock commemorating where she had grown up. "It might have been only a rock to you," I reply, "but to me it was an adventure in Eatonville. That was a great trip."

This one is even better. We are looking for the homeplace of reclusive Southern writer, Harper Lee. At 8 p.m. the two-lane road off of the interstate is without light of any kind. Trees rush right up to the pavement and stop, gnarled and snarling, waving ominous arms. It occurs to me that if we were to run out of gas (we won't), have car trouble (I hope we won't), or be stopped by some rogue posing as a sheriff, we might be in serious danger.

I am remembering lines from Truman Capote's "A Christmas Memory" that describe the young protagonist Buddy's cold march through these very woods in search of whiskey for fruit-cakes from Mr. HaHa Jones's honky-tonk café.

We make it into town, get a hotel room, and in the morning tour the courthouse where Harper Lee's father tried cases, the balcony from which she watched him as a child, and, of course, the Truman Capote / Harper Lee museum and gift shop. I wonder how Ms. Lee feels about having *Mockingbird* memorabilia spread across Monroeville.

The locals embrace her these days as beloved, and that must feel good to her on Sunday mornings when she and her sister stop in at the local Hardee's for coffee and biscuits. She is beloved by me, too, though I've only met her through written words.

Before we leave the court square, I cannot resist a visit to the Monroeville post office, where I drop her a carefully penned note. I tell her that she has been an inspiration to me most of my life, not only because of the characters and values of *To Kill a Mockingbird*, but also because of her example. Both she and Capote remind me that even in the heart of a provincial Alabama town, miles off the interstate, insulated and insular, genius and a different way of seeing and thinking can spring up like moss roses in pavement—unexpected and beautiful. Deep, rich spirit sprouts in all kinds of places.

Mentally, logically, I do not expect a note back from Ms. Lee, but my breath draws in a bit as I sort through the envelopes and fliers snatched hastily from my mailbox days later. What do I expect? What affirmation do I await—that she can feel a connection to me, too, someone she's never met, never read, who merely shares a background similar to her own?

I do not think a letter will come, nor, I suppose, do I need one. Sometimes people light the way for us and never know we're there. Sometimes just being who they are and doing what they do is enough to keep the ominous woods at bay.

Montgomery, 2011

IT'S SUMMER, AND ALL of Alabama is steaming, scorching, sizzling. Five white women from Indiana stand in front of a new restaurant in historic downtown Montgomery, sweltering and waiting for my once and future friend Delores Boyd. We have agreed to meet on our way to Florida, but I have had a hard time finding my way here, and I do not recognize the street we are on.

Delores has brought her friend Vanzetta McPherson, another former federal judge and partner in Roots and Wings bookstore. Van seems cautious at first, but we all quickly plunge into the inevitable educational, social, and political discussions that exhilarate us. We thaw to one another and swim in idea soup.

After lunch, Delores and Van show us around the renovated downtown. We walk to the circular fountain on Court Street, the center of the city, and my memory yawns awake. Isn't this the fountain in which Zelda Fitzgerald swam on one of her scandalous adventures? I suddenly remember coming out into the cool late fall evening with the sun slipping beyond a nearby building—my childhood dance studio! I hardly recognize the brick façade; all of the buildings have been revived. The city is pristine.

Across the street is the department store where my grandmother shopped with me. Farther down is the site of my first job wrapping Christmas presents. When was that? I couldn't have been more than thirteen years old.

We pass the old Whitley Hotel. Isn't this where my brother took the bar exam? I'm not sure of anything, but Delores and Van are. Yes, the Whitley was once the venue for law exams. They show me the site of the new library that Van's husband, Thomas, is helping develop. We walk to the Rosa Parks Museum, and Delores points to the spot where Ms. Parks boarded the infamous bus before the Montgomery bus boycott rattled a city, state, and nation, shaking loose an avalanche of determination and change.

Both Delores and Van have been involved in the Rosa Parks Museum and the historical archives. Van has been an assistant attorney general for the state of Alabama and active in family law. They take us to the Southern Poverty Law Center, and I dip my fingers into the water of the fountain at the Civil Rights Memorial. I trace the names of people who gave their lives in the struggle, names carved into the rounded sculpture. The water pouring from monument's stone seems somehow soothing, as if justice has finally found its way home.

Both Delores and Van have been instrumental in shaping this city. It seems like their city, a place they have earned and built, have fought in and fought for.

They take us to the church where Martin Luther King preached, and only two blocks away, the church of Ralph Abernathy, where Delores and others were shut in and threatened during the Freedom Rider protests. I was miles away in my white church, St. James Methodist, where—can this possibly be an accurate memory?—football great Bart Starr's father acted as a deacon when blacks were turned away from our service. This was a church where Lurleen and George Wallace attended services, where we were a confused and struggling people.

We have lived in two worlds, Delores and I. Her Montgomery has been horrible and beautiful and substantive and rich. My Montgomery has been suffocating and so bewildering that I have walked away.

And it has followed me.

The Rocker

TONIGHT THE WIND BLOWS in tantrums, and the leaves collide and scatter across the deck. Alone in this uneasy dark, I walk through the house and switch on lights. I open the door to the spare bedroom, the room that once belonged to my son, and there, in the pale light of the moon, the little wooden rocker sits empty. Gold plates glint on the back of the cherry wood where I have affixed these reminders: Jeff, 1958; Zach, 1983; Annie, 1996.

I can barely remember the perfect truth of this, but I think the rocker originally belonged to Jeff, my brother, the first child I loved and "mothered." By the time Jeff was born, our mother was perpetually tired and frazzled, and so I strolled him about, lugged him around in a wagon, dressed him in doll clothes, and wrapped him in ketchup-soaked bandages for a lark.

Most nights when he was a baby he cried. My mother spanked him. He cried louder until surely his lungs would burst. I dared not move. Cowering in the night, I waited for the morning when I would lift him out and hold him.

I knew nothing about mothering at age nine, but I loved Jeff with a sentimental and ever-forgiving love, and I picture him now perched on the edge of his dark wooden rocker, thin legs dangling, Popsicle dripping onto his knees. In the moonlight I touch the edge of the rocker where the crease of his knees once met the wood. In the muted moonlight, I am circled by photographs, real-and imagined.

When I became a bona fide mother to a boy decades later, I still knew very little about mothering, a role that never came easily. But loving was natural and effortless, and so I held the little boy and danced and sang to him, always trying to do the right things, whatever that seemed to be on any given day. When he was old enough to sit in the rocker, I'd place him there and read *Where the Wild Things Are* and Dr. Seuss. He listened, even if he didn't love the cadence and words and stories quite as much as I did. On Christmas Eves, I recited e. e. cummings's story poem about a little tree brought in from the cold. "Indulge me," I said. "I'm shaping tradition."

But Zachary grew too old for rockers and stories, grew into a wild thing of his own. I was sure the chair and some part of my heart would have to be wrapped up and put away; I missed him so. Some part of me knew he was off and running, as I had been . . . our time together forever altered.

But before the rocker could be dragged into the attic, my friend Jamia adopted a little girl, and miracle of miracles, I grew to love Annie, too. The chair became hers.

For adventure, Annie and I went to the donut shop, to the mall, to the bookstore, to the beach. We perched in oversized, slip-covered chairs in rented beach houses, our shells resting on the windowsill, our books resting on our laps.

Three children, spaced years apart, wrote notes in childish scrawl professing love, and I have saved them all. "I always have faith in you," reads one slanted line. "When you need a happy face, you know I am here."

Just last week, cleaning out my bookshelves, I found a card from Annie. The Hallmark verse reads, "On this day for celebrating love, I want to thank you for teaching me so much about it." But wasn't that lesson also taught in reverse, and haven't I been the learner?

Author Barbara Kingsolver writes, "Memory is a complicated thing, a relative to truth, but not its twin," and because I know she's right, I save notes and photographs to bear true witness. I engrave little gold plates and fasten them to a cherry chair to record the history of its children.

This is the role we play for those we love; we bear witness to the importance of their lives—in stories, in letters, in memories recorded. When the wind sends leaves scraping across the screens, when the night narrows in, we hold up recollection (like a flame) to give us light.

A Certain Slant of Light

I AM STANDING at the kitchen window when I realize this early autumn slant of light is reminiscent of something that has touched me deeply before, but I can't say what.

The light elicits slivers of memory—like stained-glass shards that somehow should fit together to form a unified mosaic. The pieces try to arrange themselves: the slant of the sun, the toast just finished, the begonia I bought and planted yesterday because it reminded me of my mother, a call I received, an unexpected gift . . . they are connected in this moment of reverence and realization, but I don't yet see the pattern. I don't know how or if things are connected in an understandable way.

I move to a different window to try to catch the import of this sensory input, to hear or see what is speaking to me. Yellow floats sideways across the glass, yellow that is either leaf or finch. Soon birds won't come to the feeder—not again until spring. Their coming and leaving seem sporadic, and though I understand cycles, the unvisited feeder seems permanently abandoned.

In a piece by essayist Annie Dillard titled "A Field of Silence," the author describes just such a moment as this. She pauses in a deserted field, close to touching something she can't explain. She ends the piece by writing, "There are angels in those fields, and I presume in all fields, and everywhere else. I would go to the lions for this conviction, to witness this fact. What all this means, about perception, or language, or angels, or my own sanity, I have no idea."

I have been worried about my son's search for an apartment in a safer part of New York City and touched by the concern of friends who have called to offer help. They don't have to bother, but they do because they have children of their own. We are all concerned about safety and connection, and we huddle together around the hope that we can help not only ourselves but each other.

When I was a child I felt safest in the presence of my maternal grandmother, a hardworking woman who fed me chili and cheese toast and wrapped me in a red satin comforter before a gas heater on Friday nights when the weather grew cool. She is gone—like my mother—but sometimes I sense a presence from them both. I wonder if I'm naively superstitious or incompletely intuitive.

As it turns out, just last night my son found a rather expensive place for himself in a safer part of town. I have slowed down enough today to let that sink in. I don't know who helped to make that happen—angels on the ground or elsewhere, or maybe happenstance. What all this means about friends here or gone, perception or my sanity, I have no clear idea, but in this moment I revisit the possibility that there is a network larger than myself. In this slivered slant of light I feel the fragile prospect of clarity and the possibility of connection.

Changing Season

IN MIDTOWN MANHATTAN, light falls across Bryant Park like a shawl, sideways—graceful and askew. The sun's thin rays trail along the ground like fringe, tangled in ivy and sweet potato vines.

The green and gold of October nestle in the park against New York City's Public Library, and benches of readers, of old friends, of lovers and children, scatter all across the park. Noise from the street is softened by foliage.

There in Bryant Park, I gaze up at a cloudless square of Indian summer sky, framed with yellow leaves and the glass and chrome of skyscrapers. The moment is tranquil, perfect—suspended there in warmth and light between the last of the summer impatiens and the first of fall flowers. I sit amid a spectrum of colors, planned in pots all along the walk, and feel a balance before boarding the plane for home.

At 7 p.m., through the window of the airplane I see a New York harbor. Both the sun and the moon are visible—a sunset, moonrise on this weekend when one season spins into another. A turning point. A putting to rest of a certain barely definable season . . .

With no small sacrifice, I have flown here to the Northeast to help my only child move, buy furniture, rearrange his physical life—the result of a promotion. I am proud of his hard work. When I look into his eyes, I see my own at twenty-five—not the same color, but the same poignant intensity. I have done two things I set out to do a quarter century ago: relate to him in a genuine, human, connected way and be there for him no matter what the circumstance. In other things, I have surely failed him, as he tells me in one of our calm conversations in the cool of the evening.

"In many ways you didn't prepare me well," he says. Surprisingly, his words cause me to smile. I said them, not aloud of course, to my own mother dozens of times. He is the same idealistic and critical and hopeful person I have been. Why aren't things, why weren't things, perfect, he wants to know.

I failed to prepare him well in the same way my mother let me down because children don't enter the same worlds their parents knew. They don't have the same dreams and priorities. Kahlil Gibran wrote that our children's "souls dwell in the house of tomorrow, which [we] cannot visit, not even in [our] dreams."

In recurring dreams I have had this picture: My son is standing before me, not yet school-age, dressed in a green plaid suit. He has on a dapper hat, and he holds both of my hands. "You look beautiful," I tell him. "But it's chilly," he says. "Is this the right suit for the cold?"

In my nighttime dream, I realize I haven't thought of that. I have been too taken by the beauty, the artistry, the aesthetics of the moment and the relationship.

Waking, I realize that my days of gathering and sugaring flowers for cakes with a toddler, my nights of beautiful books and stories, the perfect Christmas ornaments, the lessons in honor and love, probably left little room for more practical instruction.

But, still, will my lessons and love be warm enough when certain inevitable winds come his way?

Enough. My time for dressing him to face the world is over. I have done my flawed best. Now he must face the world with instruction that comes only from the recesses of his own mind and memory.

And I must face this changing season when instruction is done. Through the window of the plane, the sun has set. The moon has taken over, and the calm light of evening is restful and promising in a way I can't quite name.

Hope

ON THE CUSP OF AUTUMN I have gone for an early morning drive, and the leaves promise change, dangling as they do in patches of red and yellow among the green. The air is too cool for my summer T-shirt.

The radio interviewer remarks on the election of Obama, the historic moments, and suddenly I am crying. Audibly. Anyone passing can see me, and I realize I must look strange with my halting intakes of breath. I am picturing the beautiful daughters of Barack and Michelle Obama and knowing that forty-five years ago they could have been in a despised, bombed church instead of on a stage with confetti and praise and honor, and I am full of unexpected emotion. Do whole cultures evolve? And do they shed cumbersome, ill-informed loads, like animals losing useless fleece and fuzz?

Emily Dickinson wrote that "hope is the thing with feathers," the thing that lifts and rises. Hope that we can move inward, forward, and upward is startling in its possibility. My tears are a response to something so deep and meaningful that I have no place to categorize it. And in my lack of full understanding, I simply cry. When I try to put words to feelings, I realize that the Obama presidency closes a circle of hope that I started drawing around me when segregation began falling away all those years ago in an Alabama high school.

Like feathers, the leaves float down against my windshield, dry and gentle, like comfort, and I accept this catharsis for myself and for a country in need of wisdom and change.

Get Out before It Blows

THREE WEEKS BEFORE Thanksgiving and the sky is summer blue, the air sweater weather. Gusts of wind rise and pop like the starting gun of a marathon, and leaves fly off like so many runners chasing past one another. The limbs are bare with the exodus.

A week passes, and freezing rain swirls where leaves were tumbling only days before. An old familiar sense of loss shuffles in with the cold, and a guilty dread of the holidays hovers.

I know I am not alone with this indistinct anxiety that accompanies the afternoon shadows of November. I am not the only one who is quietly calculating just how short the holidays will fall when measured against a Norman Rockwell ideal of harmony.

Things change, age, dissolve. I empathize with friends missing loved ones who were here only a short time ago. I observe others trying to make sense of injuries or illnesses that have descended unfairly, unexpectedly. With a sense of disquiet, we join some vaguely agreed-upon holiday dance, swept up in patterns and traditions, often feeling as if we have somehow missed the center and are whirling about the periphery alone or incomplete.

When I feel thusly dispirited, I remember one of my favorite Story People drawings by Brian Andreas. In it, knobby characters with orange and yellow bodies jauntily assemble around a turquoise center pole, considering the possibility that life is not fair. It seems as if one character has departed, and another remains, left behind. Below the turquoise pole, in vertical marks, someone has been keeping score. An angular blue character explains that "life is more fair than we can ever imagine— if we are there to live it."

He means, at least in part, that whatever losses we sustain were preceded by the fullness of a joy or love that made the perception of loss possible. He wonders if we can make ourselves aware of the joys when they actually surround us.

On this eleventh day before Thanksgiving, the lesson is not lost on me. Before the temperature dropped to twenty-five degrees, there was this one perfect day with sun and wind in my hair, an auburn dog by my side, and the leaves chasing down a sloping green hill. I was fully present. The image remains, and I take the strength and beauty of it with me.

I take another Brian Andreas sentiment with me, too. In this Story People drawing, a smiling, color-drenched character holds a sign written in childlike scrawl proclaiming, "Rules for a Successful Holiday: 1. Get together with the family. 2. Relive old times. 3. Get out before it blows."

Revived by Water

30A

IN WARM SEASONS on the North Florida coast, dusk crawls in, barely moving under the weight of heat. Slight circulation from mosquito-driven air creeps across porches in the still hour before dark.

Down the beach road to Grayton, the scent of pine rises from the wetlands. Frogs and water creatures punch soothing holes in the coming-night stillness, and the sun throws up dying hands. Gold and pink nails scratch the western line of trees.

Five more miles and the sand and clay roads of Seagrove wind through oleander and scrub oak, and the pace of life slows to a pastel yellow . . . like sun or honeybutter pouring over life. Wisteria and jasmine climb trellises to the sun
and I am home.

One Particular Harbor

FINALLY I HAVE AGREED to take students to Italy at the insistence of my colleague, Attilia, who believes I am too provincial. Attilia is a strong woman, independent, intelligent, and self-reliant. She is equally at home in Italy, India, Germany, or China because she's an ardent traveler with a strong sense of self.

I have a strong sense of self, too, even if I am more provincial. I can be capable in unfamiliar places.

Today the sun tags the window and reflects across a string of olive trees that borders the narrow road. In the distance, abandoned farmhouses stand in brick and plaster—gold, orange, and coral—appearing and disappearing as the tour bus follows the long curve of the Apennine Mountains.

Italian vineyards wait for summer in expectant rows. I can't know when the foliage will appear in this unfamiliar terrain, in this springtime in Tuscany. Today I can only imagine America, where forsythia blooms as it does here outside of Florence. Azaleas must be blooming there, too, half a world away. I lean here against an Italian tour bus window, my iPod plugged into Yo-Yo Ma and solitude. I realize with regret that I'm one of those ethnocentric Americans, accustomed to wide-open spaces, excess water, and gas-glutton cars—one of those Americans who needs Cokes with ice and hot coffee to go.

For this week, of course, I'm willing to drink cappuccino in glass cups, standing around a table in a roadside cafe; I'm willing to be "ecological" and "Continental," not wasteful at all, but I'm not thrilled about the Italian norm of no food or drink on the run. A Smart Car buzzes in and out of lanes along the highway, zipping around the big tour bus like a dogged fly. These

Italians are economical and feisty. They're beautiful, like their architecture, their leather, their glass, and their art. No doubt about that. A few of them have even been friendly.

My Italian traveling mate, Attilia, translates for me, giving a direct kind of sass right back to any clerks who are impatient with my hesitation and confusion. She's at home here, though she's been away from Italy for many years. She points out mimosa trees that line the side streets, full of yellow puffs. They remind her of her childhood, she says. Her voice is wistful, but only for a moment.

I have been thinking about Robert Frost and his silken sonnet. This is what I have learned about myself: "Strictly held by none," I am "loosely bound by countless ties of love and thought." It is only when the wind blows, Frost says, when the ties go taut, that we realize how we are gently but inevitably bound to others.

It has been cold here in Italy, and though I am with friends, the wind off the Adriatic Sea has made me long for the radiance of my closest kindred spirits. With them, I can always find what Ernest Hemingway calls my "clean, well-lighted place," a safe place in the bright light. They are basking along the Florida coast.

Jimmy Buffett names this phenomenon of familiarity and peace "one particular harbor," that one pleasurable comfort zone where soul mates convene and the weather, both physical and emotional, is, to some degree, predictable and manageable.

This is, I think, what we work for, what we seek, all our lives—this region in the heart that feels like coming home.

Enchantment

THERE'S THIS BALCONY overlooking Scenic 30A that's serenaded by frog choirs and palm fronds. Across the street, turquoise water lies flat against white dunes. For most of my year I dream of these days on 30A. At home, I wake facing a stressful task, look out across a Midwest winter landscape, and think only of sun, shells, and sea. This is the ideal. The dream.

At the beach, I have a 6 a.m. routine: I flip-flop over to Tom Thumb, get coffee and head across the boardwalk in search of shells, always with the same childlike expectation. For my second dose of caffeine, I head down Highway 30-A, the stretch of beach road that I claim personally, although I have no deed to prove ownership. Here I feel a soul connection, and souls require no real estate.

When the sun first curves across the sign at Seagrove Market, I continue past Dogwood and Azalea, counting one by one the lanes of curved oak and palmetto, making my way to Modica Market.

At Modica I purchase a sausage biscuit for ninety-nine cents. Under hand-lettered signs, vacationers line up for ambience and waffles. The shelves stack to the roof, and sliding ladders sidle up to Merlot and rare Shiraz. But I'm not thinking about wine. I loll about, sipping coffee and waiting for the Sundog Books to yawn awake and let me in. When it opens, a black Labrador blocks the entrance, and I step around.

My first morning on the coast, I find two novels and a dozen tiny shells (one so small it sticks, hidden, to a dime orphaned in the bottom of my cup)—a delicious find on the books, but a disappointment on the seashells. I spread the modest shells on the sill to dry and forget for a time that they are there.

One late afternoon, when the fresh exuberance of being at the beach has mellowed into midweek comfort, I begin to study the shells that have amassed in the window. Some, tainted and broken, I discard, but of those that remain, I notice that the first shells gathered, the dozen or so fragile baby shells, have taken on a nuance of shape and color in early evening light that reflects coral, rose, lavender, palest yellow, and cream. In the long, transient twilight, I have time to notice that everything along the sill is rich in form and texture, an ample harvest.

It may be that we have to make it to a certain time and place in early evening to recognize the richness of all we have collected.

It may be that enchantment is acquired.

Lesson

THIS YEAR THE ENCHANTMENT is short-lived. I have chosen to spend a week alone at the beach before anyone else comes down. I have anticipated this for months. I have awakened in the gray cold of February with my face against a stack of pillows and stared at aged limbs, imagining the beach, warm and white, edged in turquoise. I've envisioned the sun as a feather boa, falling across my shoulders in the dappled warmth of beach lanes.

For three days now, I have been alone here—free to walk and think and write. But in the reality of "my perfect place," the dream has formed a hollow center. I have written all I have to say. I have checked my email dozens of times a day. I've fashioned gifts for friends who will arrive in four more days. I have weighed the balance of what I need from myself and what I need from others.

I cannot seem to find the formula for connecting the introverted writer to the friend who lives life enough to have something worthy of writing.

The most disturbing revelation of all is that the beach with all its sun and magic is not a perfect palliative. The exquisite is replaced by a disquieting shadow that wags its amorphous, shapeless finger at the idealist, at the dreamer in me.

With the arrival of those I love, the beach becomes again a haven, an escape, but the magic of the place has been replaced with the magic of the people, and I am grateful, grateful, grateful.

July / Kentucky

THE RAIN THAT FALLS evenly on this July night in Kentucky is unlike any rain that I remember. I walk through the dark listening to the rhythm—neither a drizzle nor a storm nor a mist. The rain is slow, like the speech here, drawn out and soothing.

I've driven past lakes and flatland, raccoons and produce stands, to get to a literary reading where one author reads (with love and humor) about a backwoods cousin who lives in a doublewide out in the hinterlands. I know for a fact that this author has animal heads on her own rustic walls and lives above a barn.

Here in the southwestern corner of Kentucky, I've met a twenty-eight-year-old who says the Pulitzer Prize "don't mean nothin'" and a sixty-year-old who began her literary life two years ago after raising seven children and living a hard life in the Kentucky hills. This reading has attracted an exotic dancer, a music groupie, a Mennonite minister, and a paralegal who works in the Chicago office that once employed Michelle and Barack Obama. They are all here to listen and to learn, bound by the common love of the power of storytelling.

Constance, a sophisticated New Jersey transplant who has lived for twenty-two years in this small Kentucky town, reminds me that this is the fiftieth anniversary of the publishing of *To Kill a Mockingbird*. In Monroeville, Alabama, other literary types gather to celebrate what CBS has recently announced as the "most inspirational book of all time."

It is the inspiration that keeps us going back for more of the oral and written tales told well. It is the link we find to that cousin in the remote doublewide, as well as to the woodsy author who relates his story. We all have—or are—the strange cousin.

We all know Boo Radley and Tom Robinson and narrow-minded townspeople by the dozens. We all have a story that we are living—and dying to tell.

There is a license plate here (besides my own) from Vanderburgh County, and it belongs to a University of Southern Indiana instructor whom I never see in Evansville. But here, miles from home, she admits to me that she's started her own novel, beginning "with a very steamy online chat with a lover." Slightly embarrassed, she says she's set the tale aside. "Resurrect it," I say.

Amid the tattoos, Hawaiian shirts, horn-rimmed glasses, Republicans, Democrats, feminists, good ol' boys, vegetarians, Catholics, atheists, quilters, and banjo players, I sit listening, rapt, to the story of Jamie, his two girlfriends, three dogs, and one doublewide. How rich and varied is the weaving of the tales we live. Outside, the rain raps on the roof like so much applause from the muses.

Spiral

I SIT ON THE BACK porch until the sky is almost black, and still no storm. A dog barks far across the way. Frogs chant, bugs hit against glass, and night sounds remind me of a childhood when fireflies rode the white steam rising from July pavement. The history we live when we are young takes years to process and decode, but we always come back to it.

The sky in the west spreads east into deep purple. Leaves catch the wind and travel off against a night sky that promises rain after a season of scorching heat, unending.

In this drought, I have been hoping that "to everything there is a season." The weather has taken its toll physically and emotionally. Plants, animals, and people wilt in the heat, and we all wait for change.

My Southern biblical roots haunt me occasionally, and verses surface and whirl. Raised with scripture and fried food, I can't escape the imprinting. One who is "trained up in the way he should go" may depart from it, but she cannot travel so far that she outruns the memories or the habits. Given a choice of pleasure or duty, I almost always choose solid Methodist duty. Given an option of organic oatmeal or fried chicken with biscuits, I'll go for the latter and add a Coke. Given oppressive heat, I sit and wait.

I am beginning to understand that whatever is planted in a spring season—be it physical, emotional, mental, or spiritual—remains to some degree. I think this is true of outer places as well as inner spaces.

A basic Jewish prayer talks about teaching children well. A Muslim friend shares this Arabic saying: "If you learn something when you're young, it's engraved in stone." Truths resurface in every culture and subculture, wearing slightly different symbols or wording. We are shaped by home. We are molded by homeplaces.

In such a mobile society, moving from place to place throughout decades, we leave multiple lives behind. The little red icon at the top of the Facebook page invites us to remember them, to come face to face with old lives and almost-forgotten places, rediscovering the people in them. What we see can be complex, layered with conflicting feeling and memory, both joy and regret.

Because of social media, I have reconnected with eighty-seven thousand of my closest friends through Auburn football. I have relinked with students I taught thirty years ago, and we remind each other of what we read and said and meant to one another. I have regalvanized bonds with junior high school friends who meet yearly at the beach. Eighteen women my age fly or drive from around the country, and we find even more in common now because of age and experience. We have learned to judge less and listen more. One of these friends is Peggy Wallace, who has walked across the infamous Selma bridge hand-in-hand with Civil Rights icon John Lewis. My friend Delores writes me that she and Peggy have recently had a most substantive talk.

T. S. Eliot writes that at the end of "all our exploring" we arrive where we started and "know the place for the first time."

We grow and change—certainly. We outrun prejudice and increase sophistication. We throw off aspects of provincialism just as a child throws off constricting clothes and shoes when summer comes. We expand.

But lurking in the center of who we are lie the roots of who we have always been. In times of grief or stagnant drought we revert most deeply to those roots, hoping to tap water. If we arrive where we started with some sort of insight, we can finally see a common thread that travels through all we have been and done.

And after every literal or figurative dry spell, rains and richness eventually revive us and we realize that life is more than just a circle that closes back upon itself in so many repeating patterns. Inevitably comes a spiral, a moving onward and upward. This is the promise I hold onto within every drought.

Fully Present

OCTOBER 1962. THE ALABAMA sky is clear, and the sun, no longer direct and unrelenting, curves around the trees. Noon sunlight falls across Mason jars of camp stew, lined along folding tables with spreads of barbeque. The band plays brassy football songs across a junior-high field, and cheerleaders wave green and white pompoms to stir the midday heat. There's a young U.S. President, but everyone around me dismisses the whole Kennedy clan (just a bunch of Communists) with frustrated sighs: "What's this country coming to?"

In 1968 crickets sing in syncopation to soul sounds across a midnight campus. October nights in Auburn are heavy, like blankets. We hardly have time to think about Bobby Kennedy or Martin Luther King, Jr. because we're too busy dancing after every ballgame to the sounds of Otis Redding and Sam and Dave. No campus protests here, but my deepest spirit often feels disconnected with the way I live.

Five years later and autumn rides the Florida air like a whisper, barely there. Young men come home broken from a war I hardly know. They are trying to survive, and I am trying to do the same.

By 1986 I have a little boy to wrap in vest and hat against the October chill. He rides a pony for Halloween all across the Tennessee hills, and I carve pumpkins and bake cookies, working two jobs to pay a mortgage with interest rates in double digits. My neighbor lends me a book about the economy and imminent disaster, but it rests unread on my screened-in porch.

1988: I am moving north, displaced from all I have known. For two decades I have written that Southern rules and tradition, politeness and narrow boundaries, nearly smother me. But these things melt into my veins and are my lifeblood, too. So what do we do when we face a bloodletting, when we have to let go? If not let it go, at least relegate something in the past to a different or lesser position?

By 1993, I am a divorced mother who thinks deeply in moments snatched from the rush of everyday living. My son is so independent he doesn't need me for October trick-or-treating. He's part of a motley crew, a happy-go-lucky neighborhood gang, complete with dogs and sabers and scythes—all manner of Halloween accoutrements. President Clinton has just passed a Budget Act to deal with runaway deficits, and the Republicans are restless for a change. Not much time to consider that... I snap a photo, and here, now, I hold it in my hand—a tin man, a ghost, Robin Hood, a hobo, and my happy son, growing, growing...

Grown. October 2009. The sky is pure blue. Starbucks has pumpkin spiced latte, and the trees are persimmon, gold and peach. I catalogue October images, falling all around me like confetti: green and white, orange and blue, midnight black and sunny-yellow. A young U.S. President wins a Peace Prize and the undercurrent shakes and grumbles. Exactly what's this world coming to? I have adored this man, this President, not only because of his intelligence, but because he has closed an open circle for me. Justice has come, and some of the wounds of the last century are healed somewhere in my heart.

Seasons spiral and scatter events we haven't the time, education or inclination to process respectfully. Too busy, we go about our lives with only half a mind open, only one ear pressed against the world, even those of us who consider ourselves thoughtful. What would it mean to balance personal survival, social consciousness, and selfish/unselfish actions and behavior?

October 2012. Forty years since junior high school. The autumn rain hits soft against the screen in my first full autumn out of school. I have retired from teaching and have time to think, and what I think is that wisdom means being fully present, finding balance between introspection and extroversion, between involvement and solitude.

November / Delivery Delayed

THE WIND AND RAIN have begun to blow winter in. Persimmons cling to bony limbs in a late afternoon November light.

I know this light, a light peculiar to Indiana, a herald of Thanksgiving. I've studied it now for twenty-three Novembers. I'd know it anywhere. Dropped blindly into a Midwestern field, blindfold removed, I'd smell the air and notice the bark on sycamore and birch and know the third week of November by the slope of the light.

The rain is the comforting, promising rest now that a quicker, fuller season has passed. A life that is too wide and rushed cannot be deep and reflective. I am glad to slow down, to take joy in the small moments as well as the major passages.

Last Sunday I went to a baby shower, bearing baskets of gifts and such sincere good will for my friend, her daughter, and her new grandson-to-be. The women who celebrated the impending birth spanned generations, all seemingly gracious in accepting the season in which they found themselves—mothers with children on the way, mothers with children still in school, and women with empty nests, remaking their lives. Happy to be included, I wrapped myself in the joy of the moment, the champagne and laughter, never consciously admitting to myself how much I missed my son, never daring to articulate that we might never have any similar traditional celebratory event in any branch of our unconventional family.

At the close of Sunday evening, I received a call instructing me to add Skype to my computer. Then, there on the screen, Skyped from Argentina, I saw my handsome son, hair disheveled, greeting me unexpectedly. He wanted me to meet his beautiful fiancée. Across the miles, through technology, I became a part of a long-imagined vision of all I had hoped for him.

And so this, too, is a cause for thanksgiving—that seasons change and beauty is found in the most unexpected places and the most unexpected times. My good friend, a writer and actress, has begun to attend a church with a charismatic minister who calls to her from the pulpit: "Sometimes delivery is delayed!" Indeed it is. We expect something on one day and it comes to fruition, fuller than ever imagined, years later.

The wind and rain have blown November in. I am quietly grateful and have come to think that perhaps it is true that to everything there is a season, and a time to every purpose under heaven.

Wild Sweet Orange Ride

THE WATER ALONG the Florida Keys is turquoise, banded with purple. Mangroves rim the road, arms outstretched, begging alms. I give them awe.

We are driving to Key West, four people in a rental car, loudly discussing politics, religion, writers, and film. The arguments are heated, but soothing, because the four people in this car agree on the basics and debate for sport. We pile thoughts and details atop one another in a thickening blanket of ideas. We warm each other with raucous feigned disbelief and amusement.

In the car are two old friends I've known for decades and see maybe once every five years. My son, whom I haven't seen for a year and a half because he is busy building a life in New York, is there, too. We pick up with no lapse. I'm deeply grateful for that. Here we are in neutral territory—not my house, not his, not theirs, traveling down U.S. 1, a road with water for a curb.

These two old friends remind me in private that my duty as a parent is to enjoy my son. No more lessons. No judgment or reining in. Here in the indolence of the Keys, amid understanding and laughter, I find the right time and place to make the shift.

When we get to Key West, we walk the streets, sampling restaurants and bars. We amble up steps to Fat Tuesday, an outdoor bar, and the greeter checks my son's ID. "You need to check *her* ID," my son jokes. "She's my date."

"Dude, she's your mother," the greeter retorts. "You look just like her." We have good laughs.

In the morning, in the sweet orange sunlight, we go for breakfast at Pepe's, a Key West landmark near the docks. On white weathered boards, peeling signs inform us: "Since 1909—Under Old Management."

I'm charmed. The bougainvillea falls over our table in fuchsia and green drips. Locals sip coffee, and the French toast comes with blackberries, fat like dimpled thighs. For days we take photos of food: French toast, Brie with guava jelly, tropical drinks.

We have no map, but at least one of us has had much experience on the road that threads the Keys. Traveling back, we stop to balance on a rusted bridge over Florida Bay in Bahia Honda and to take photos of Sea Grapes arching like awnings over dusty paths. I catch my son in the lens of my camera as he, too, photographs pathways and inlets—a perfect picture.

We snap photos to hold on to these warmest of moments. The metaphor of a rental car leaping key to key—across water, possible sinkholes, and bridges of varying reliabilities—is apt. After all, what do we truly possess on this larger journey, this adventure without a map, except a few unconditional friendships, a few like-minded people in a car? It is a wild sweet orange ride, this weekend, this life. . . .

Finding
Air

Union Street Impressions

STREETS CLANG WITH deliveries and bikes, and just below the metallic clink, languages mix and tangle. Buckets of flowers stack outside of Brooklyn corner markets, and strollers rattle along uneven sidewalks. Silver scooters send children with backpacks sailing up toward Prospect Park, and just beyond the iron fence, four floors up into the summer air, the plant in your window curls to the light

 that seeps down the brick
   onto Union Street.

Brooklyn Homeplace

SPLAYED ACROSS THE CHAIR, color photos in the *New York Times* entice me from just above the fold. The snapshots are slick and summoning, in lime and persimmon inks edged with exotic fonts.

I purchase the six-dollar bundle of glamour and mystery because my son and his friends stroll across page four in a happy parade of style so far from all I have known and been that I marvel at the trajectory that landed him in New York's "Sunday Styles," frolicking about in the Easter parade.

I measure the twelve years since my son left home in hours of missing him, in quantities of time and money I have willingly offered up in whatever ways I could—always seeking to affirm, but not interfere. I constantly try to envision the life in Brooklyn that he so treasures.

Last April, next to me in a Starbucks chair identical to mine, lounged a friend who had returned to Indiana after years away. She, too, had seen the *Times* photos and responded with appropriate awe. More than a dozen years ago she was a student of mine who loved the novel *Their Eyes Were Watching God*, and, like the heroine, Janie, she walked out of Evansville with her eyes focused forward, never looking back. Until now.

She tells me she is still considering her options, trying to find or remember a place that fits. She says the eerie calls of coyotes across woods on the west side of town soothe her in a way she can't explain.

Today I am trying to corral my thoughts of utter amazement about how life unfolds, to wrap the wildly floating bewilderment in some kind of mental Spanx, to reel it in. But my incomplete understanding, my inability to make sense of how each individual is propelled through this life, spreads, refusing to be easily ordered. What makes a homeplace of where we land?

We ourselves—or our children or nephews or friends—make decisions, move from one stage of life to the next, float away, bound for locations encoded mysteriously somewhere in DNA and daydreams. We leave behind people we have loved, their hands metaphorically lifted, sending us out with only a memory of when our hands rested in theirs.

In youth we rise up, testing winds with our energy and fresh beauty, caught in currents we can't possibly predict. From some distance, it is difficult to see that even the most capricious and bold airborne kite is tethered by a barely discernible string.

My son, who landed in Brooklyn in 2001, watched the Twin Towers fall from his daunting, horrifying perch on the Brooklyn Bridge. He walked the streets of Williamsburg and Park Slope, wandering the pubs and art galleries, marveling and making a place for himself until finally he fell in love with an Australian doing the same. They married, standing under the arch of his beloved Brooklyn Bridge, and I rejoiced in her beauty and understanding of him, in his courage, independence, and boldness. Brooklyn is his community, he says, because in it he has made his mark and built the space around him; he has been able to make a difference. Brooklyn is where he has stopped and stayed because "some familiarity and safety and acceptance felt like home."

He has now built and owns a bar and restaurant with three other partners, and he goes, every day, where "everyone knows his name."

My young friend, next to me in her leather chair, only one year older than my son, proposes that a homeplace requires "a sense of community and purpose, where we find others who see the best in us."

A homeplace happens when we stumble upon a community where we are so filled up that we spill over in a cycle of giving that returns to us and perpetuates itself. In the comfort of a homeplace, we can be captured unaware, frolicking about in living color, doing whatever it is that we were born to do.

Ballast

IN MANHATTAN, THE afternoon rain rests in waxy relief on fruits stacked on the vendor's sidewalk cart. Behind the cart, a city park, lush green and fenced by iron railing, strikes me suddenly as an image too complex to process in passing. I am walking quickly, and the sounds of the road splash and honk on one side of me. With so much sensory input, I can only file away the image, like an imagist poet, before the moment is gone.

On every corner the smell of coffee wafts into the wet air, soggy and heady, delicious and rich, and I am drawn into the Plaza Deli, on East Forty-Fourth Street, out of the rain, into the aisles of color and smell. It has been a spring and summer of delicatessens for me, stores in other cities offering food for fast purchase. There is something nonthreatening about going alone into a deli in an unfamiliar city, getting lost in the shoppers, and finally ordering just a pastry, a drink, a slice of cheese to carry out, unwrapped. I move about, invisible.

Markets boast fat orange shrimp, cooked and tempting, next to even brighter orange pimento cheese and Italian breads, cranberry and orange muffins, stacks of cans climbing the walls and exotic bottles bearing names I've never seen, all exhilarating and tiring, stimulating and baffling.

Here, near the corner of Forty-Fourth and Second, in a city so different and distant from home, I find myself thinking of what home really means. When did I grow confident enough to wander deli aisles alone and carry inside of me a piece of every place I've been and everyone I've loved—a montage of a ballast?

Home from New York

YESTERDAY, ON AN OVERCAST Saturday morning, I pulled my muddy Jeep into the gas station across from the Hornet's Nest bar and eatery, far out into the country, and climbed out to buy coffee. Home after weeks away, I was soothed by the simplicity of a stop at a favorite crossroad. How I love to worship at the temple of the familiar.

I have been fundamentally changed by my time away. Driving south through my hometown, I found my great-grandmother's house on Finley Avenue torn down and replaced by a defunct industrial or automotive business of some sordid sort. Unable to locate my grandmother's grave in the cemetery nearby, I learned that she had chosen to separate herself from her extended family and cast her lot with an old friend somewhere beyond the boundaries of our family graves. And her house, where I spent almost every Friday night as a child, had fallen into such decay that I could barely look at it, and so I drove on. No amount of softening or rewording will alter the reality that time passes and order alters.

A week later, flying north and witnessing my son's beautiful marriage, I realized that he hopes to build a family that will somehow escape the complexity of the families we both have known and loved. His new family will be made up of multiple ethnicities and cultures, and so I can only imagine that complexity and challenge will find him, too, as it finds all of us. Writer, psychiatrist, and spiritual thinker M. Scott Peck suggested that we should strive to embrace the multifaceted, the intricate and composite, that we need to abandon the urge "to simplify everything, to look for formulas and easy answers."

Instead, he proposes that we "begin to think multi-dimensionally, to glory in the mystery and paradoxes of life, not to be dismayed by the multitude of causes and consequences that are inherent in each experience—to appreciate the fact that life is complex."

Sitting outside in the warm air, I talk with a friend about what it means to appreciate complexity—to come to terms with great joys and monumental losses: a house erased, a gravesite lost, a loved one far away who will probably never move back. My friend comments on the hybrid roses lining the iron fence beside us. They bloom again this year in a profuse, rich summer red and seem to be invincible, but they somehow seem too thick of stem, too tough and thorny, too rigid. A Knock Out Rose, bred to escape all turmoil, cannot possibly look or smell as sweet. I prefer the slender bend of a rose that has survived mildew and beetles and gone on to bloom precariously.

No matter how we try to package all that is complex and fragile into an ordered, understandable, indestructible whole, maturity teaches us we cannot tie up all loose ends, control all messages, alter all outcomes. It's good to be home, but good to venture out, too. To be open to the unexpected and the irregular, to the inevitable surprise, yields its own form of wisdom, and, I suppose, eventually, some sort of inner strength and courage and comfort.

Indiana Summer

ON THIS LATE SUMMER evening along Indiana Highway 57, every lawn has been trimmed evenly, and fields stretch for miles, falling off into forests in the early dusk.

I am moved anew by the ordered calm of the rural Midwest, especially since this sunset journey follows a recent trip through the Deep South where yards withered in the tired heat—where road construction bordered miles of crawling traffic on boiling black asphalt. Passing through Tennessee and into Kentucky, I began to cool down.

It is good to be home this evening, to feel as if I belong to this place—finally, after more than two decades living here. The winding road of rustic landmarks proves to be the best of tonics.

We have lost our fourteen-year-old Sheltie, and our family is off-balance and inconsolable—no one more so than our one-year-old Retriever mix who rides in the backseat, sticking her nose out into the wind. The scenery is comforting, but our mission is serious and sober: Should we seek a canine sibling so soon?

I have convinced myself that we do not have to rush to find a new companion. When we reach the farmhouse where possibilities await, I am cautious and reserved, as are the puppies who run under every shelter possible, most notably the garage, to protect themselves from the ninety-pound yellow dog that bounds out of the backseat.

The woman who owns our prospective new family member is unbelievably patient and gracious. She walks the rolling acres with us, letting Maia, our dog, swim in the lake and roll in the mud. The pretty little runt of the litter follows Maia fearlessly, the lone pup brave enough, curious enough, to play.

By the time the last of the sun has dropped into the woods that surround the farm fields, we have decided to take a chance. The little retriever is not a Sheltie and not the most gorgeous of the group, but she is small, pretty, and brave, and I cradle her in my arms as she sleeps all the way home. Then I cannot know that her bold bravery will translate into shenanigans too bizarre to believe as she grows older.

Maia, too, falls into an exhausted heap in the backseat, and the night slowly darkens from blue to black. I think that this moment, gliding through the summer night, ranks right up there with other simple, favorite, miraculous pleasures—the joy of a good book, the smell of morning coffee, and the comfort of a loyal hand to hold, a feeling of belonging.

We decide to name the pup after the dog in a movie we love. When I search online for the meaning of her name, "Brinkley," I find this: "field in the forest; woodland clearing."

I am an incurable and unapologetic romantic. Could anything be more nearly perfect? This will be a dog for all seasons, of course, but burned into my mind is a sunlit snapshot of two dogs running across the meadow toward a country lake in the last light of an Indiana summer day.

Birthday

IN THE SHORT PASSAGE "Eleven" by Sandra Cisneros, the youthful narrator, Rachel, says, "The way you grow old is like an onion or like the rings inside a tree or like . . . little wooden dolls that fit one inside the other, each year inside the next one." She goes on to say that "when you're 11, you're also 10, and nine, and eight and seven, and six, and five, and four, and three, and two and one."

That's why Rachel says that on our birthdays, all the previous years rattle inside us "like pennies in a Band-Aid box."

This week is my birthday week, and the realities of age eight are, indeed, clinking around somewhere inside of me; I am a third-grader, lying in bed, worrying that I will grow old, perhaps making it to age forty.

Thank goodness, I made it past my forties, and I still run, dance, do yoga, sing Bruce Springsteen songs flamboyantly with all the car windows down, wear big hoop earrings, and take the occasional dare. I like to walk barefoot at the beach, wear short skirts, and drive convertibles and Jeeps, just as much as I like to read books in solitude, take naps, and engage in other age-appropriate thrills. If I look at myself objectively, I am often surprised that the twenty-three-year-old I remember does not show up in my photographs or in the mirror. Who is the woman with laugh lines and furrows creasing her skin?

If I lean in really close to the mirror, I see my insecure thirteen-year-old self, my overly emotional sixteen-year-old self, my stubborn and defiant eighteen-year-old self, and my thirty-two-year-old nurturing new-mother self.

The memories, the feelings, the behaviors stack inside me

like plastic chairs, one on top of the other, all visible from the sides and the back, if not apparent from the top looking down.

I am bewildered by aging and time. As Rachel says, "All the years inside of me are pushing at the back of my eyes," and I'm trying to see the line that separates the "me that was" from the "me that is." I see no line, only a continuum, and I need words to construct that paradigm clearly. I see the girl who danced with wild abandon at twenty-three. She's still in there somewhere, and I need my own permission to lift her out at any time. The forty I imagined at age eight was not the forty that I lived. The sixty that I am has no gray hair or bad knees. The trick must be to erase the old images and replace them with what has actually come to be.

I'm sixty today, and fifty-nine, and twenty-three, and thirteen and eight. Sixty is wiser than twenty-three—and more assured, calmer, more stable—so, all in all, I'm thinking that life just stacks up, gaining depth.

The Watch

IT IS LATE IN DECEMBER, at the end of the evening, and the light from Droste's Jewelers beckons. Good. The shop is open. An elaborate wooden door leads into a flurry of activity that mimics the movement of villagers rushing around at the top of a clanging cuckoo clock.

I have come on a mission of the heart, and in a box tucked inside my backpack I have my grandfather's twenty-one-jewel pocket watch, nestled in a padded box. A Westside jeweler has restored it to beauty, and I have come to Droste's now to have it engraved, a gift for my son.

I step tentatively to the center of the store, and around me people bustle about in muted holiday light. When the gentleman behind the counter offers to help, he is so open, natural, and uncondescending that I am surprised. I can be shy in jewelry stores, sure that whatever business I have come to complete is trivial compared to the errands of others who have enough money to make a real impression. Tonight I consider again the power of money to shore us up and give us confidence—or to make us hesitant and unsure.

This is no small town where customers know the shopkeepers, and I do not know the gentleman's name. He is tall and gregarious, jovial and full of life. "This is a beauty," he tells me, gently handling the chain. He reaches for a book and reads the number inside the back of the watch. "It was manufactured," he tells me, "between 1935 and 1936."

"It was my grandfather's," I say. "He was a conductor on the L&N Railroad."

"So was my father!" he exclaims, and he shows me how the

conductors wore the watch fobs, just so, holding the Waltham watch against his buttonhole. Clearly he loves his job here. He tells me more about the watch and takes precious time with me as other customers circle around in last-minute holiday shopping. We are suspended here together in the gentle light of the shop, clearly connected by what we love—he his craft, and I my son.

I cannot know how much money this man makes, whether he owns a financial interest in the store or merely owns a personal interest in watches and jewelry, but it occurs to me that this type of passion for one's craft, this type of knowledge and love of a job might be passing away in an increasingly impersonal and technological job market, one in which the drive to make money sometimes trumps one's interests. In the current world economy, just having a job often has to be enough.

What would happen if everyone, like this craftsman, followed his or her curiosity and passion?

We would then, I think, hand down to our children and grandchildren, in addition to elegant physical objects, a centeredness and peace—a model to emulate—a hub, a heart, a core.

Begging Bowl

ON MY DESK IS A GIFT, a hand-thrown Buddhist begging bowl. The lesson of the begging bowl is that what we need will come to us—that at the end of the day our bowls will have been filled.

I tell others—and I honestly believe it, despite my own tendency to worry—that we are only channels through which money, time, love, and energy flow; what we give out comes back to us again. There will be enough.

I have placed the glazed begging bowl on my desk to remind me of my basic "channel" belief that rests somewhere within my core. Every night before bed I realize that—for that day—I have had enough. The lesson is reassuring.

Exploring the history of the begging bowl, I found that the Buddha divided what was put into his bowl into forty-nine portions that sustained him on his way to enlightenment. Once enlightened, he threw his golden bowl into the river, having no need for possessions.

I am hardly so evolved. I need my bowl. I like looking at it.

For several years I left the bowl empty to remind me that it waits, every day, to be filled, and every day it has been. Lately I have added to the bowl prayer beads (a gift from the Middle East) and a printed poem written by a friend's mother, "Cling to angels, touch glory, remember miracles, speak peace."

In the end, these essential things matter: what we have given to others through relationship and what they have given to us, what is beautiful to see, to hear, to feel.

In the company of the hand-thrown sea-green pottery bowl, wrapped in sun on the edge of the desk, in the presence of the perfect poem centered in the middle of the swirls and shades of green, I practice serenity.

There is This

IN QUIET MOMENTS we consider what we treasure, even if we can't bring ourselves to speak the list aloud.

There's the scent of the coffee shop, the deep confidence of belonging to people who love us, the Friday night at home with a book and a Coke in a very small bottle.

There is the crispness of new sheets after a long, formidable task, completed well, with no responsibility stretching out ahead, only rest.

There's the song that comes on unexpectedly, bringing a wave of remembering. The dance when no one's watching, the symphony when the cello is pure, the performance when the singer has a voice that never falters.

There is the curved orchid, reflected in the mirror, the maidenhair fern lifted and moving on a slight wind. The child who surprises us with a card or a visit, the young person who stops by with a meaningful realization or confidence.

There's the one perfect sentence that catches us unaware and lifts off the page, circles around the brain and drops back, faultless, in black on white. The poem that moves across the mind like a cat settling in, familiar. The rounded white shell. The pale rose, opening. The dog curled quiet before the fireplace. The friend who understands. The cotton quilt. The morning spent shopping for someone's gift. The taste and smell of bread.

There is the first day at the beach when, not even checked in to the beach house, friends jump from the car and sink bare toes into white sand . . . the driving south, giddy with expectation, watching the temperature climb—fifty degrees, sixty, sixty-four, seventy-five. The candy allowed on a trip, but no other time—Mary Janes and caramel. The seagull that drifts down like a billowing ribbon and lifts off again against the sun.

There's New York movement and light, the vibrant pace, the scarf bought on the street, silken and of colors so beautiful they ask to be painted.

There's the first spring mowing, late in the afternoon, with the sounds of children on bikes and the smell of grass and promise; the wild warm wind through an open car. The gaze out an autumn window at hills of sweater-color leaves, the scarlet cardinal perched on an arching fence in early snow.

There's the way life curves back on itself to make sense of what seemed senseless. There is justice that rises out into the light, even after so long a time . . . so long a time. There is the friendship that grew from almost nothing into a grounded, solid rock to light the way to understanding.

There is this and so much more in this rich life to remember with quiet thanks, to appreciate with eyes and spirit open, even if we are reluctant to count aloud the moments for anyone else to hear, even if we are reluctant to throw them onto paper, to send them skittering across a page. . . .

About the Author

JULIA HIGHTOWER GREGG is a writer, teacher and founding member of Signature Consulting, educational and writing consultants. She is also a founding member of Signature School, a public charter high school consistently ranked among the top schools in the country. She teaches International Baccalaureate English part-time at Signature School and is a columnist for the *Evansville Courier and Press*.

Ms. Gregg has a BS from Auburn University, an MS from Vanderbilt Peabody College, and an MFA from Murray State University. She lives with her family, including two overindulged Golden Retrievers, in Evansville, Indiana. *Wild Sweet Orange Ride* is her first book.

About the Artists

ARTIST JANICE GLASS WILLIAMS is a friend of the author since late childhood who paints from her home studio in Perry, Georgia. Her contributions to *Wild Sweet Orange Ride* include the nature images done in oils and pastels.

LINDA WAREN GOODRIDGE, who contributed the paintings of beach house and bookstore, is an artist, former art teacher, and resident of Mt. Vernon, Indiana, where she is involved with community arts, her children, and grandchildren.